D0879783

A *Joiful* MOMENT

Finding Joy in Life's Tough Places

JOI THOMAS

A Joiful Moment: Finding Joy in Life's Tough Places
by Joi Thomas

© 2018 by Joi Thomas

Published by The Church Online, LLC

For information, address the publisher:

The Church Online, LLC
1000 Ardmore Blvd.
Pittsburgh, PA 15221

International Standard Book Number: 978-1-940786-62-9

Library of Congress Catalogue Card Number: Available Upon Request

First Edition: February 2018

Trademarks

Foreword

The lines from the poem, "Life," by Paul Lawrence Dunbar speak to the experience of so many persons. To name a few:

"A crust of bread and a corner to sleep in,
…A minute to smile and an hour to weep in…"

Life is difficult and confusing. Often persons feel as if they cannot and will not make it. In fact, many have concluded that this is just the way life is meant to be and it is the best that they can do to just keep on going. I have seen it in the disappointed faces of little children and distant stares of adults looking off to a faraway place so different from their present.

It is to those struggling with these emotions and those feeling as if life has dealt them an impossible hand that Joi Thomas has penned this devotional work. There is a way through the maze of the difficult. There is a path through the uneasy places of life and it is God who creates the path, gives the light for the path, and equips us with the strength needed to walk the path. You are invited into *A Joiful Moment* so that you can be with God and let the love of God do its restorative work.

As a lead radio personality, Joi has been a blessing each and every week from her perch at the WEAA radio station in Baltimore. Now, her words have been put in a form that can minister to all of us. It is a privilege to read these words and be blessed with the inspiration Joi evokes. As Joi's Dad, I have seen that joy come alive in her and now she shares the thoughts God gave her with each of you.

Take this thirty-day journey with *A Joiful Moment*, and you will be *Finding Joy in Life's Tough Places.*

Bishop Walter S. Thomas, Sr., Pastor
New Psalmist Baptist Church, Baltimore, MD

Introduction

Life is a continual journey of high and low moments. There are times when you are happy and excited about what's to come. There are other times when you are terrified and scared of what the next moment will bring. It is in these times that you wonder if you will ever recover, or if life will ever get back to normal.

Over the past four years, I was in this place—a rollercoaster ride full of highs and great lows. I suffered many personal losses, and I wondered if life would ever get back to a place I recognized. In the span of four years, I had a miscarriage, had a baby, went through a separation and then a divorce, and grieved the sudden death of my godfather.

Many days, I just pushed through to get back to my bed, only to start the cycle all over again the next day. The pain was often overwhelming, and I would pray each day that God kept me healthy. I prayed that He wouldn't let the weight of the stress have an adverse effect on me. I was in a fog. However, deep inside, I knew that it would get better. I would sing the chorus of Vashawn Mitchell's song over and over again: "It won't always be like this, God will perfect that concerning me. Sooner or later it will turn in my favor, it's turning around for me." On the days where it was hard to get out of bed, I told myself it wouldn't always be like this. On the days when the tears wouldn't stop, I told myself that sooner or later, it would turn in my favor.

With much prayer and love from my family and close friends, the tides began to change. I felt my strength come back, and I felt my focus return. I could hear God's voice clearer than ever. His conversations with me shifted from those of sustaining to those of prospering. He began to give me a new dream and a renewed purpose. I could see my way out of the emotional storm I was in. A new Joi was emerging—a stronger Joi who fully understood God's sustaining power.

God kept me through the worst storm of my life and confirmed everything that I had ever learned about Him. You see, I grew up in church. My father is a pastor, my mother is a deaconess, and my brothers preach. I know God. I was taught who God is at an early age, and I watched as my parents served Him and led others to Him. I was trained in my faith, so when the storm hit, even though I didn't think I was, God knew I was prepared to withstand it. He held my hand every step of the way, and sometimes He just held me and let me feel what I needed to feel. He put people in my path who encouraged me and showed me that life goes on. He took care of my son when I didn't have the energy to do so. Above all else, He reminded me that there was power in my name, Joi, and that His **joy** would sustain me and give me strength. Even when I hit rock bottom, I was okay; God's **joy** permeated through me and reassured me that all would be well.

My prayer is that this devotional will remind you of the **joy** that God gives, the **joy** that will sustain you through life's painful moments. The **joy** that won't allow you to give up on God, but give you the strength to wait on Him. The **joy** that will heighten your senses and allow you to see where God is working in the midst of your chaos. Each entry will give you a scripture for the day, a message to meditate on, and a prayer to pray. Just as I do on my Sunday afternoon radio show, "Gospel Grace," during my Joiful Moment segment, each day I will also recommend a song for you that will reinforce the theme of the day's devotional; music always helps me feel closer to God, and I hope it helps you as well.

Now, I ask you to dedicate yourself to this process. Make sure you take time each day to spend with God, and get in tune with the **joy** He has placed within you.

Day 1

THERE IS NO NEED TO FEAR

Isaiah 41:10 (NIV)
So do not fear, for I am with you;
do not be dismayed, for I am your God.
I will strengthen you and help you;
I will uphold you with my righteous right hand.

Fear is a human emotion. Even Christians experience fear for one reason or another. Isaiah 41:10 reminds us that there is no need to fear. God is always with you. When going through life's most difficult situations, it's easy to forget that you are not alone. One of the byproducts of trials and tribulations is loneliness. Your mind will trick you into believing that no one cares, no one will be there for you, no one loves you, and the list goes on. This simply isn't true. Even if no one else is there, God is always there.

You may say, "But I can't feel him or see him!" I would encourage you to take a deeper look at your situation. God is most definitely working out the details. Sometimes, God fine-tunes your situation so much that you have to use a magnifying glass to see just how much He is working. Remember how you were sad about all you were enduring, and your favorite song came on the radio? For four minutes you forgot about your situation because you were singing at the top of your lungs. Or how about the time you were at the end of your rope—ready to give up—and out of the blue someone gave you an encouraging word that spoke directly to your situation? It could have been a total stranger that told you to have a good day, and in this particular instance, you began to believe that you would have a good day. See, God doesn't always do big things to get your attention. Sometimes He works in the details to make sure you aren't alone and that you have a solid foundation to grow from. So, I admonish you not to be afraid, because God is with you. He will strengthen you. You have no reason to fear.

Prayer

God, thank You for always being by my side. There were times when I couldn't tell if You were there or not. The storm clouds were so thick that I couldn't get my bearings straight. I couldn't see. I now know it was You steering the boat, making sure I didn't get lost in the storm, or worse, go overboard. Thank You for never leaving me. Help me to grab hold of this promise today and in the days to come as I work my way through my present trial.

In Jesus' Name,

Amen

Listen To: "No Reason to Fear" by JJ Hairston and Youthful Praise

Thoughts and Ponderings

_____

_____

_____

_____

_____

_____

_____

_____

_____

_____

_____

_____

_____

_____

_____

_____

_____

_____

_____

_____

_____

_____

_____

_____

_____

REMAIN STEADFAST

James 1:12 (NIV)

Blessed is the one who perseveres under trial because, having stood the test, that person will receive the crown of life that the Lord has promised to those who love him.

While you are going through a storm, the hardest thing to do is persevere. It literally takes every fiber of your being to make it from day to day. Sometimes you can't even imagine making it through the entire day. When I was at my lowest, I asked God to help me make it through the morning, then to help me make it through the afternoon, and then the evening. My situation was that heavy, and I was that overwhelmed. Thinking about it now brings tears to my eyes. However, God has an answer to every tear that you shed.

Today's answer is found in James 1:12. Apparently, I have been chosen to be blessed because I persevered through my trial. A quick search of the definition of persevere turns up results such as: "to maintain a purpose in spite of difficulty, obstacles, or discouragement; continue steadfastly" (dictionary.com). Imagine going up against insurmountable obstacles with no chance of survival or success. It's a daunting task, and yet God says after you have stood the test you will receive the crown of life that the Lord has promised to those who love Him. I like to think that this crown is something we will experience here on earth, and not just when we meet Jesus on the other side. To me, this crown represents peace, wholeness, and clarity. Because God promises this, it is then a given that He will make sure it comes to pass. Remain steadfast through life's most difficult moments. When it seems hard, stay resolute and stay focused on what you are facing, and in God's time you will receive the crown of life for your perseverance. It will be worth it.

Prayer

Dear Heavenly Father, this weight is so much to bear. Each day that I am faced with the same situation, I feel more and more defeated. I need Your help. Give me the strength I need to remain steadfast. I have no idea when You will change this situation around for me. All I know is that You will do it because You promised me that You would. Help me hold on to this promise, even in my darkest hours. Help me to have faith when I don't see the outcome, and God I promise You I will give You praise even now because I know that You will keep Your word.

In Jesus' Name,

Amen

Listen To: "Hold On Old Soldier" by Mississippi Mass Choir

Thoughts and Ponderings

_____

_____

_____

_____
_____
_____
_____
_____
_____
_____
_____
_____
_____
_____
_____
_____
_____
_____
_____
_____
_____
_____
_____
_____
_____
_____
_____

Day 3

GOD CARES FOR YOU

1 Peter 5:7 (NIV)
Cast all your anxiety on him because he cares for you.

Newsflash! God cares for you! Yes, you, He cares for you and all your faults and mishandlings. It is a trick of the enemy to believe that God has left you all alone in your situation. This is far from the truth. He is right there, and when you are going through those rough moments in life, you need to be reminded that God is with you, and He cares for you. You may ask, "How can God care about me when He allowed this to happen to me?" The answer is simple: God's concern for you is not based on anything that you have done or anything that has been done to you. He cares because He is God. He created you and always wants what's best for you.

I'm sure there are numerous reasons why you find yourself in your current situation. Whatever the case may be, God is here and He cares. He knows the hurts and pleadings of your heart, but He wants you to give them to Him. He wants to form a relationship with you and make you stronger at the end of this trial. Remember, whatever we face in life is ultimately so that God will get the glory. I urge you to give your situation to Him today. Have an honest, frank conversation with God. Tell Him how you feel. Tell Him what you cannot tell anyone else, and watch Him begin to work things out.

Prayer

God, I am scared. There is so much going on in my life, and I can't see straight. I can't tell if I'm coming or going. I feel so alone in this—alone with my thoughts and feelings, alone with the reality of my life. So God, I need Your help. I'm leaning on Your word right now which tells me to cast my cares on You because You care for me. God, please help me to feel that care and concern today. I desperately need to feel You in the midst of my trial. Send me a reminder today to help me keep moving forward in this trial. Through it all I love You and I trust that You know what's best for my life.

In Jesus' Name,

Amen

Listen To: "He Cares for You" by Rev. Milton Brunson

Thoughts and Ponderings

_____

_____

_____

_____

_____

_____

_____

_____

_____

_____

_____

_____

_____

_____

_____

_____

_____

_____

_____

_____

_____

_____

_____

_____

_____

_____

_____

_____

_____

_____

_____

_____

_____

_____

_____

_____

Day 4

YOU CAN DO THIS!

Philippians 4:13 (NKJV)
I can do all things through Christ who strengthens me.

God has given you the power to overcome any situation. He gave you the perfect example in His son Jesus. If Jesus can overcome the grave, surely you can overcome whatever you are facing. In fact, Jesus gave you the power to do even greater things than He did. I know that what you are facing seems insurmountable. I know. I've been there. Sometimes the pain and confusion can be so crippling that you literally can't move. You feel stuck, not knowing what to do next or which direction to go in. Life's hurtful situations take all your energy. It takes everything in you to keep going from day to day—just to keep yourself stable. Then, you use energy to care for others, to be productive, and to process what you are dealing with. It leaves you weak. The good news is that this scripture is the answer you need to keep moving. You can do it. It may hurt, but you can do it. You must do it. For every believer, there is no other option but success. We are representing God our Father, and He never fails. Stand up, wipe your tears, and begin walking toward your solution. You can do this!

Prayer

Dear Heavenly Father, first and foremost, I want to thank You for bringing me this far. It has not been easy, but I am aware that I would not have made it if You were not a part of my life. I'm at a sticking point and I feel weak. I don't have the strength needed to continue with this present situation. God, please stretch my faith today so I can operate in Your word. I know You have given me all I need to succeed and be victorious. I need reminders of that today. I want to be an example for You even through this present trial. I love You, Lord. I'm grateful that in spite of what I'm dealing with, You have given me strength to see it through.

In Jesus' Name,

Amen

Listen To: "All Things Through Christ" by Earnest Pugh

Thoughts and Ponderings

_____

_____

_____

_____

_____

_____

_____

_____

A Joiful Moment

_____

_____

_____

_____

_____

_____

_____

_____

_____

_____

_____

_____

_____

_____

_____

_____

_____

_____

_____

_____

_____

_____

_____

COUNT IT ALL JOY

James 1:2-3 (NKJV)

*My brethren, count it all joy when you fall into various
trials, knowing that the testing of your faith produces patience.*

This scripture seems like an oxymoron. It's telling you to count it all joy when you face trials. How can that be? How can you remain joyful in the midst of the hardest moments of your life? How can you be joyful when you are enduring pain? How can you consider it an honor to go through life's trials and tribulations? Honestly, this requires enormous faith in God and His promises. In order to remain joyful in life's difficult times, you have to believe and trust the God who told you to do so. It's typically against one's nature to stay positive during difficult moments. However, God commands us to. He even tells us that this testing produces patience, and patience is the key to enduring any situation you find yourself in. The unknown is what makes hardships so difficult. However, patience will help you stay in your right mind while you are in the midst of crazy circumstances. Remember, you are patiently waiting on God to solve the problem, remove the problem, remove you from the problem, or strengthen you to endure the problem. All these situations require you to patiently wait on Him to do His work. I know, it may sound crazy, but remember that the testing of your faith produces patience, and being patient will give you peace. Count it All **Joy**.

Prayer

Dear Heavenly Father, I thank you for another moment to talk to You, and cast my cares on You. I am going through a rough time right now. In fact, I am in the fight of my life. I am doing my very best to look at my situation as You have commanded me to. I am trying with all my might to see this as a blessing. I know in the end, You will get the glory. Help me to remain joyful amid this. Please God, with all the devil has attempted to take from me, please don't allow him to take my **joy**. Help me to face this trial with Your **joy**. Help me to be cheerful when I want to cry. Help me to smile when I feel like frowning. Help me to put my faith in You, while You produce in me the patience I need to endure. God, this is hard, and I am scared, but I trust You with everything I have to get me through this.

In Jesus' Name,

Amen

Listen To: "Count it All Joy" by The Winans

Thoughts and Ponderings

_____

_____

_____

_____

_____
_____
_____
_____
_____
_____
_____
_____
_____
_____
_____
_____
_____
_____
_____
_____
_____
_____
_____
_____
_____
_____
_____
_____
_____

Day 6

DO GOD'S WORK

1 Corinthians 15:58 (MSG)

With all this going for us, my dear, dear friends, stand your ground. And don't hold back. Throw yourselves into the work of the Master, confident that nothing you do for him is a waste of time or effort.

When you are going through a rough situation, it's common to seclude yourself so you can process your thoughts, think things through, lick your wounds, and so on. This scripture tells us to do the exact opposite. When you are dealing with life's heavy situations, it's not the time to sit back and be shy and wounded. Instead, God commands us to stand our ground and continue to do His work. Now is not the time to run away from your work in God's church. Do the exact opposite. Continue to do the assignments God has given you and allow Him to minister to you as you work for Him. Nothing that you do for Him will be a waste of time. Nothing that you do for Him will be in vain. God has a purpose for everything. Don't stay isolated. Please don't. It may be hard for you, but your spirit needs fellowship. So drag yourself out of bed and make it to church. Instead of going home straight from work to watch the shows on your DVR, go to Bible study. I know you just want to go home and go to bed, but don't do it. Go to choir rehearsal. You will be surprised how much God ministers to you while you do His work.

Now God didn't say be phony or lie and say that you are doing well; He just said that you should throw yourself in His work. You don't have to have it all together to be about His work. Be honest with those around you. God is the master architect, and so often his plans make little sense to us, but once He is done, a masterpiece is built. You have to trust Him and follow the outline that He gives for making it through life's difficult times. He needs you to be visible during your trial because others need to see your strength to know that they can make it. I know you may not want to hear this, but it's not all about you. Stand tall, don't back down, and do God's work while He works on you.

Prayer

Dear Heavenly Father,

Thank You for this day. Thank You for waking me up and starting me on my way. Today, I need You to fight for me. The spirit of isolation is real, and right now I don't want to be around anyone. I just want to be alone. I don't feel like plastering on a smile just so others will feel comfortable with my trials. Give me the strength to be honest about my struggle while serving You. Help me to not feel ashamed or influenced by the opinions of others, but rather revel in Your strength. I know that the devil wants me alone with my thoughts, but I need to hear from You right now, God. Turn the volume of my spiritual ear up so I can hear You, and give me the strength to hold my head up high while You work this out for my good.

In Jesus' Name,

Amen

Listen To: "It Pays to Serve Jesus" by the Aeolians of Oakwood University

Thoughts and Ponderings

_____

_____

_____

_____

_____

_____

_____

_____

_____

_____

_____

_____

_____

_____

_____

_____

_____

_____

_____

_____

TRUST GOD

Romans 15:13 (NIV)

May the God of hope fill you with all joy and peace as you trust in him, so that you may overflow with hope by the power of the Holy Spirit.

Let me paint a picture for you. You are going about your day as usual when you get the phone call that changes everything. Suddenly, the world and your life look different. It goes from sunny to cloudy, from warm to cold, from certain to confused. The wind of life is knocked out of you, and you are left sitting there—shattered—wondering how in the world you will be able to move on from this moment. It is a life-defining moment, and now nothing makes sense. You scream, cry, or maybe just sit too stunned or numb to do anything else. At some point, God speaks, even if you don't realize it's Him, and He tells you it's time to get up. You have to move from this point and begin again. It is the hardest thing in life to start over when you never thought you would have to. It takes strength and courage—strength and courage that you probably think you lack.

This verse provides enough power to get you moving again. When things turn haywire in your life, the first thing you have to do is trust God. You have no other choice but to trust Him. While you trust Him, He will fill you with **joy** and peace—the kind of peace that helps clear your mind and see the possibility that one day, you will be happy again. You may not know when, but day by day God's peace will help you make it through, and His overflowing hope will allow you to believe that **joy** is coming. However, if you don't trust God first, none of this will happen. You have been knocked down, but before you call your best friend, before you tell all your business on social media, before you begin to plot revenge, TRUST GOD. If you do this first, He will give you everything you need to come out of this stronger than before.

Prayer

God, I cannot believe what just happened. I keep thinking that I am going to wake up and it would have all been a bad dream, but this really happened, and I have no idea what I am supposed to do now. I don't understand how I am supposed to go on with my life. I don't even know if I am adequately describing the hurt and emptiness I feel right now. God, I need You like never before. Help me to trust You. When I want to take matters into my own hands, remind me that You are in control. I am hurt, confused, angry, sad, furious, and dumbfounded, but there is a small part of me that wants to turn all of this over to You. Help that small part grow and outnumber the human side of me that feels lost, overwhelmed, and defeated. God, speak to my unbelief and help me to trust You without a shadow of a doubt. God, I want to get through this Your way, and I will need Your help so that You will get the glory. Even in this, I thank You because I know things could always be worse. Strengthen me as I go through this storm and help me come out better.

In Jesus' Name,

Amen

Listen To: "Why Not Trust God Again" by Kurt Carr

Thoughts and Ponderings

LET IT GO

Ephesians 4:32 (NIV)
Be kind and compassionate to one another, forgiving each other, just as in Christ God forgave you.

Forgiveness is such a hard concept to grasp. It's tossed around frequently. Numerous books and websites are dedicated to helping you forgive, mostly emphasizing the point that forgiveness is more about you than who you are forgiving. Release the negative energy, don't let that person and their actions have control over you, blah, blah, blah. We have all heard it before. The truth of the matter is, forgiveness isn't quite that black and white. It isn't easy. And honestly, the deeper the hurt, the harder it is to forgive. I've learned two things about forgiveness that I hope can help you. One is that forgiving doesn't mean you forget. I can forgive you for hurting me, but I won't forget that you hurt me, and that fact may alter how we move forward. The second thing is, as a Christian, you sometimes have to just do what God commanded because He commanded it. Today you may not want to forgive that person who caused you tremendous hurt, but because God has outlined that forgiveness is the way to go, start working on it. He didn't say it would happen instantly, but if you trust that He will give you the strength to forgive, one day it will be sincere.

Forgiveness is a process, and it will take complete trust in God and in His plan for your life to go through it. You can do this. Let it go.

Prayer

Dear Heavenly Father,

This walk is hard. Not only have I been hurt, but You have stated that Your will is for me to forgive. God, how am I supposed to forgive the person that literally crushed my heart into a million pieces? How am I supposed to forgive the person that betrayed me? How am I supposed to forgive the person that lied to me? God, only You know just how deep this pain is. There are days I can barely breath from the pain, and now I have to forgive? In order to do this, I am going to need Your help. God, give me the desire to forgive, and then send the resources to help me work through my pain so I can forgive. I know forgiveness is a part of Your plan, and if Jesus can model forgiveness during the greatest trial of His life, I can work on it through the biggest trial of my own. In spite of it all, I thank You for what You are doing, and what You are going to do in my life.

In Jesus' Name,

Amen

Listen To: "A Heart that Forgives" by Kevin LeVar

Thoughts and Ponderings

_____

_____

_____
_____
_____
_____
_____
_____
_____
_____
_____
_____
_____
_____
_____
_____
_____
_____
_____
_____
_____
_____
_____
_____
_____
_____
_____
_____

Day 9

BE BOLD

Hebrews 4:16 (KJV)

Let us therefore come boldly unto the throne of grace, that we may obtain mercy, and find grace to help in time of need.

Since childhood, we have been taught manners and how to be respectful in all situations. I'm sure you have heard many of the same things I heard growing up, like use your inside voice, speak when spoken to, don't sing at the table, be humble, always say thank you, and the list goes on and on. The funny thing is, when you are going through rough patches in life, you often have to put good manners aside and go boldly to God and let Him know the matters of your heart. I recently heard a preacher say that in order for your prayers to be important to God, they first have to be important to you. Show God that what you need from Him is of the utmost importance to you. That may mean you have to cry and shout and yell to show Him how serious you are. That may mean you begin to spend extra time with Him daily to address your concerns and hear His feedback. Whatever method you choose to use, be bold about it. Do not approach God timidly. Your present trial may have taken all your strength, but muster up a little more to go before God. The word teaches us, right here, that you will find mercy and grace in your time of need, but you must first Be Bold!

Prayer

God, I come before You as boldly as I can. I'm in trouble. The weight of my situation is literally taking me out. I can't see which way is out, and I need Your help. God, I am at wit's end, and it took every ounce of energy I had to even speak to You. I went back and forth about praying to You because You already know my situation and You know how it will turn out, but I'm calling on You because just saying Your name gives me strength. God, I need to talk to You today. Please come see about me. God, I beg You to help me see You in my situation. Right now, I have no one but you. GOD, DO YOU HEAR ME? I NEED YOU! HELP ME! I won't make it without You, and I want to make it, so *please* God, sustain me through this and give me whatever I need, because I don't even know what I need right now. I just know to come to You and let You take care of the rest. God, I've placed it before You, and right now I cannot do anything else but wait on You to answer. I have nothing left to give, so please take care of those depending on me right now while I wait on You.

In Jesus' Name,

Amen

Listen To: "Hear My Prayer" by William Murphy

Thoughts and Ponderings

_____

_____

_____

_____

Day 10

WAIT

Psalm 40:1-3 (NIV)

I waited patiently for the Lord;
he turned to me and heard my cry.
He lifted me out of the slimy pit,
out of the mud and mire;
he set my feet on a rock
and gave me a firm place to stand.
He put a new song in my mouth,
a hymn of praise to our God.
Many will see and fear the Lord
and put their trust in him.

When life knocks you down, the hardest thing to do is see new possibilities. The situation takes your focus and vision away. All you can see is what you're going through and what you are dealing with. It takes all your energy to make it through the day, but right here, in the book of Psalms, God assures us that we won't always be in that place. God will lift us out of it. However, we must wait patiently for Him.

What does patiently waiting look like? I believe it looks like a lot of praying, honest communication with God about your feelings, and asking for His direction and presence in your situation. Waiting patiently means that you do not shut yourself off from loved ones and friends. You fast and study God's word. You are vigilant about hearing God's voice, knowing that He is going to answer you. God is going to firm you up, and you will see things begin to settle down. It's such a wonderful thing to stand upon the rock that He has placed you on and look down and see just how far He picked you up. Better days are ahead, I promise you they are. It may not look like it now, but your **joy** will return, and God will give you a new song to sing. You will become a living testimony to others of the visible, tangible power of God to do the impossible. You have been knocked down lower than you have ever been, but watch God take you higher than you can ever imagine. Wait patiently on the Lord. He hasn't forgotten about you.

Prayer

God, I feel like You are taking forever to answer my prayer. Where are You? Do You even hear me? Have You forgotten about me? I'm here, waiting for You to make a move—because I'm human, I'm getting anxious, and I want to take matters into my own hands. I know Your plan is perfect, so I ask for Your strength to help me wait. I need Your help to do this Your way. Send reinforcements to show me I'm on the right path. God, this trial has taken so much out of me, and I feel like I'm at the end of my rope. It's taking everything in me to wait on You, but if this is what You require, this is what I will do. I trust You enough to know that my waiting is not in vain. In the midst of it all, God, You are still good, and I love You with all my heart.

In Jesus' Name,

Amen

Listen To: "I Will Wait" by Eric Waddell and the Abundant Life Singers

Thoughts and Ponderings

_____

_____

_____

_____

_____

_____

_____

_____

_____

_____

_____

_____

_____

_____

_____

_____

_____

Day 11

YOU WILL WIN

Romans 8:31 (NIV)

What, then, shall we say in response to these things? If God is for us, who can be against us?

Romans 8:31 provides the ideal response you should have when going through your current trial. Hardships come in life with a specific purpose to break you down or take you out. However, God has already given us a victorious response. If God is for us, who can be against us? I know I often thought of this as a rhetorical question. However, one day, when I was dealing with a very hard situation, I had to stop and really process this scripture. I realized that with God in my corner fighting for me, there was nothing I couldn't defeat. No matter what, I was going to win. I don't know how I will win, I don't know when I will win, I don't know how much I will have to go through to win, I just know I will win. If my victory is guaranteed, I can survive the fight. If my victory is imminent, I can push through the hardships. If my victory is a given, I can deal with the unknown. What an empowering idea this is! You may have to keep repeating it until it resonates with you. God is for me, God is for me, God is for me! And if God is for me, who can be against me?

Prayer

God, I thank You for always being in my corner. Sometimes it doesn't feel like it, but my faith reminds me that You are there. Please continue to fight on my behalf. There are times when I don't have the strength, but I find comfort in knowing that You will fight for me. I'm leaning on You like never before, God. Continue to fight on my behalf. I know that with You on my side, I will come out victorious. Help me to remember that when the fight gets harder to bear. Thank You for a fixed fight, Lord. I ask for endurance to see my victory at the end.

In Jesus' Name,

Amen

Listen To: "We Win" by Vincent Bohanan

Thoughts and Ponderings

_____

_____

_____

_____

_____

_____

_____

_____

_____

_____

_____

_____

_____

_____

_____

_____

_____

_____

_____

_____

_____

_____

_____

_____

_____

_____

_____

_____

_____

_____

_____

Day 12

GOD WATCHES OVER YOU

Psalm 121:5-7 (NIV)

The Lord watches over you—
the Lord is your shade at your right hand;
the sun will not harm you by day,
nor the moon by night.

The Lord will keep you from all harm—
he will watch over your life;

When you are going through life's rough situations, all you can focus on is the situation: the key players, the details, and when it will end. You can become so consumed by your problem that you forget that life goes on despite your situation. But it's okay; God knows, and He is watching over you. He is going to protect you and keep you from all harm. The enemy will trick you into believing that God has left you in your situation, but this is not true. Don't believe that lie. God is right there with you, protecting you. More importantly, He's not just protecting you now, but protecting your future. He is making sure that the present hardship you face doesn't destroy your future, but prepares you for it. What a mighty God we serve! Remember, God is watching over you.

Prayer

God, You are wonderful. When planning out my life, You take everything into account. You know all about me and what's going to happen next. Thank You for taking total control of my life. Thank You for keeping me from harm and danger. God, right now I ask that You continue to keep me safe as I live out this trial I am in. I know that You are a man of Your word. You said that You would keep me from all harm. I'm scared right now because of what I'm dealing with, but I believe Your word. I believe that You will keep me safe. Watch over all of those connected to me as well, Lord, while I fight my way to the other side of this. I know that no matter what, You have assured me that not only will no harm come to me, but You are with me and will be with me forever. I love You and I thank You.

In Jesus' Name,

Amen

Listen To: "His Eye is on the Sparrow" by Tanya Blount and Lauryn Hill

Thoughts and Ponderings

_____

_____

_____

_____

_____

_____

_____
_____
_____
_____
_____
_____
_____
_____
_____
_____
_____
_____
_____
_____
_____
_____
_____
_____
_____
_____
_____
_____
_____

Day 13

IT WILL BE ALL RIGHT

Romans 8:18 (NIV)

I consider that our present sufferings are not worth comparing with the glory that will be revealed in us.

There is no sugarcoating it: life can be hard. In the blink of an eye, things can go from good to bad, bad to worse, and worse to inconceivable. The pressures of life can cripple you and make it hard to move on. Difficult situations have a way of making time stand still and then slow down as you try to move forward with your life. God gives the assurance that what you are going through right now is nothing compared to the glory that will be revealed from this trial. I know the bad situation seems unconquerable, but God tells you to hold on because the glory that will be revealed will be all worth the trial. The glory that is to be revealed comes in various forms.

When I am amid a problematic situation, I like to think that the glory refers to how God will bring me out as a shining example to all. I want them to see that with Him, all things are possible. It also proves to me that with Him, I can conquer anything. I am God's glory, and when He brings me out of the situation, or sustains me in the midst of the situation, I bring Him glory by being His greatest advertisement. He gives me strength and clarity and I give Him glory. Have you ever just taken a step back from your situation and witnessed how much God worked on your behalf? You may still be in the center of the storm, but glory is coming!

Prayer

Dear Heavenly Father, I come to You right now excited about the glory that will be revealed in me. I am going through the roughest time of my life. Quite frankly, it's hard to believe that anything good is going to come out of this. I am so shattered and worn out that I cannot conceive of ever being strong again. But God, You have reassured me that glory will be revealed in me because of my suffering. My suffering has a purpose. Lord, don't let me miss Your move. I'll be here waiting on You, keeping my faith, and crying out to You daily. Please Lord, don't forget about me. I love You, and I trust You.

In Jesus' Name,

Amen

Listen To: "There Will be Glory After This" by JJ Hairston and Youthful Praise

Thoughts and Ponderings

_____

_____

_____

_____

_____

_____

_____

_____

_____

_____

_____

_____

_____

_____

_____

_____

_____

_____

_____

_____

_____

_____

_____

_____

_____

_____

_____

_____

_____

_____

Day 14

PRAY ABOUT IT

Philippians 4:6-8 (NIV)

Do not be anxious about anything, but in every situation, by prayer and petition, with thanksgiving, present your requests to God. And the peace of God, which transcends all understanding, will guard your hearts and your minds in Christ Jesus. Finally, brothers and sisters, whatever is true, whatever is noble, whatever is right, whatever is pure, whatever is lovely, whatever is admirable—if anything is excellent or praiseworthy—think about such things.

When I was younger, we used to sing a hymn in church, "What a Friend We Have in Jesus," written by Joseph Scriven. The first verse says:

> *"What a friend we have in Jesus, All our sins and griefs to bear*
> *And what a privilege to carry, Everything to God in prayer"*

I can still remember the older people in the congregation crying and waving their hands while singing this song. It wasn't until I was older that I understood the tears I saw and how this song correlates with today's scripture. Often in life's most trying times, we forget to pray. We reach out to everyone else but God, forgetting that He is the one that can help us. This scripture gently reminds us that we need to talk to God. He is the one that will give us the peace to get through the situation. Have you ever wondered why you were so calm during the toughest times in your life? Maybe you are in that season right now, and it amazes you and those around you that you are calm through it all. It is a byproduct of prayer. When you pray to God and make your requests known, He will give you the peace you need to withstand whatever you are dealing with. And then, once you have this supernatural, unexplainable peace, keep your mind on pure, lovely thoughts to safeguard your mind from the enemy. Peace is worth more than money. Don't let your thoughts lead you right back to the very thing you just prayed and asked God to take care of. Pray and rest in God's peace. It's going to be alright.

Prayer

Lord God, I come to You today fearful and anxious about what the future holds. I have no idea what to expect from life now. So much has happened, and my hope and focus are gone. My mind is racing—I don't even see how I can make it to tomorrow. God, I need You to calm my thoughts. I'm scared, and I need You. Be with me, God. Help me to see that my future is brighter than my current situation. Reassure me that You are there, and guard my thoughts so that I can focus on You.

In Jesus' Name,

Amen

Listen To: "Take it to the Lord in Prayer" by Dr. F. James Clark and the Shalom Church (City of Peace) Mass Choir

Thoughts and Ponderings

_____

_____

_____

_____

_____

_____

_____

_____

_____

_____

_____

_____

_____

_____

_____

_____

_____

_____

_____

_____

_____

_____

Day 15

IT WILL ALL WORK OUT

Romans 8:28 (KJV)

And we know that all things work together for good to them that love God, to them who are the called according to his purpose.

Say this out loud: it's all going to work out. I know it doesn't seem like it now, but God has assured you that it will. You just have to hang in there and endure the trial until God says that it's time to move on. When you face life's trials, you don't know God's timing. You have no idea when something will begin, and you don't know when it will end. This is why it's so important to cling to what you know, which is what God has said in His word. Today, we are reminded that all things work together for good. We must trust that God knows what He is doing, and one day we will see the good in the situation. This scripture doesn't speak to your present. It gives you hope in your present and speaks to your future. There is no way you could even hold on through your trial if you didn't know that God was working it out for your good. The possibilities of what God can do are endless. Hold on with the knowledge that even your trials have a purpose. Nothing is in vain. God will use every experience in your life and weave it together to create a masterpiece.

Prayer

Oh Lord, I know You have a plan. You have said in Your word that all things work together for good. I'm trusting that even this dark, lonely place that I am in will make sense one day and work for my good. Help me to remember this when things don't make sense. Help me to remember this when the reality of what I'm going through is too much to bear. Help me to focus on this truth when the devil throws lie after lie in my face. I know that in Your infinite wisdom, of which I could never fathom, this hardship is a part of Your perfect will. Today, I will rest in the knowledge that You will give my pain a purpose, and will show me that I didn't go through this for nothing. I love You, Lord, and I praise You now because I know it won't always be like this.

In Jesus' Name,

Amen

Listen To: "Things Will Work Out for Me" by Ricky Dillard

Thoughts and Pondering

_____

_____

_____

_____

_____

_____

_____

_____

_____

_____

_____

_____

_____

_____

_____

_____

_____

_____

_____

_____

_____

_____

_____

_____

_____

_____

_____

_____

_____

_____

_____

_____

_____

Day 16

YOU ARE NOT ALONE

Joshua 1:9 (NIV)

Have I not commanded you? Be strong and courageous. Do not be afraid; do not be discouraged, for the Lord your God will be with you wherever you go.

It is natural to be fearful when you are unsure of what will happen next. Being in the midst of hard times will make you fearful of what's to come. Living in fear takes its toll on you physically, emotionally, and spiritually. Fear, albeit a natural human emotion, does not come from God, and every now and then you have to put your emotions in check. God has commanded you to be strong and courageous. He doesn't clarify this statement by saying you only have to be strong and courageous during good times. He wants you to have this posture at all times. He goes further to say do not be afraid and do not be discouraged. Why? Because He will be with you wherever you go. You will never be alone because God is there, and if He is with you, there is nothing that you can't overcome. It sounds like cliché church talk, but it's true. His presence in your life and in your situation will cast fear aside. With God, there is only space to be strong and courageous. He has equipped you with everything you need to withstand this trial, and the good thing about it is that He will be there with you, right by your side making sure that your fear doesn't outweigh your faith. You are not alone! God is with you.

Prayer

Dear Heavenly Father, thank You for not leaving me alone. Thank You for always being present when I need You. I realize now that even when I felt alone, You were there, because it could have always been much worse. Build my confidence, and help me to press forward through this hardship. God, You know I am fearful of what's to come. I'm scared and I'm nervous. I don't know how any of this will play out. I just have to trust that with You by my side, I will be able to face whatever life will bring. Thank You, God, for caring about me and holding me close through all of this. I love You and I will continue to give all my fears to You.

In Jesus' Name,

Amen

Listen To: "Never Alone" by Anthony Brown and group therAPy

Thoughts and Ponderings

_____

_____

_____

_____

_____

_____

_____

_____

_____

_____

_____

_____

_____

_____

_____

_____

_____

_____

_____

_____

_____

_____

_____

_____

_____

_____

_____

_____

_____

Day 17

GOD'S GOT IT

Psalm 62:2 (NIV)

Truly he is my rock and my salvation;
he is my fortress, I will never be shaken.

It is a given that life is not easy. Funny thing is, when you are a child, all you want is to be grown so you can set the rules. Little do you know that when you are an adult, there are so many issues that you have to face. On the bright side, God is your rock. Not only should He be your foundation, but He is there as support to lean and depend on. This scripture outlines three of the ways God works in our lives. He is there for stability, to rescue us from ourselves and our sins, and to protect us and shield us from all harm. Recognizing that this isn't even everything that God is to us, but rather representative of just a few of the hats He wears, is pivotal to making it through hard situations. God keeps us stable when the world around us is shaking. He rescues us from our sins and shields us from the winds and the waves of life. He is our fortress, our salvation, our protection from the enemy. God wants us to walk through our storms with our heads held high because He is there making the crooked way straight and helping us take steps toward our future. God is going to do whatever it takes to get you through this. Don't worry, God's got it, and He will make sure you come out better than when this started.

Prayer

God, often I don't take the time to see all that You are doing on my behalf. My situation has given me tunnel vision. All I seem to see is what is happening to me and not what is happening through me because of You. It is only because of You that I am still here in my right mind during this chaos. It is only You that has restrained me from taking matters into my own hands and settling things the way I see fit. It is only You that has protected me from the forces that are working so hard to tear me apart. Thank You for laboring on my behalf and pulling out all the stops to make sure I survive this. Thank You for making me a priority and coming to see about me. I don't take it lightly that I mean so much to You. Today, I choose to praise You for how You are working on my behalf. I know I will get through this because You are with me. I love You.

In Jesus' Name,

Amen

Listen To: "God's Got It" by Rev. Milton Brunson

Thoughts and Ponderings

_____

_____

_____

_____

_____

_____

_____

_____

_____

_____

_____

_____

_____

_____

_____

_____

_____

_____

_____

_____

_____

_____

_____

_____

_____

_____

_____

_____

_____

_____

_____

_____

Day 18

YOUR RESURRECTION

2 Corinthians 1:9-11 (MSG)

We don't want you in the dark, friends, about how hard it was when all this came down on us in Asia province. It was so bad we didn't think we were going to make it. We felt like we'd been sent to death row, that it was all over for us. As it turned out, it was the best thing that could have happened. Instead of trusting in our own strength or wits to get out of it, we were forced to trust God totally—not a bad idea since he's the God who raises the dead! And he did it, rescued us from certain doom. And he'll do it again, rescuing us as many times as we need rescuing. You and your prayers are part of the rescue operation—I don't want you in the dark about that either. I can see your faces even now, lifted in praise for God's deliverance of us, a rescue in which your prayers played such a crucial part.

Your situation may have left you on the side of the road, dying, gasping for air. People walk by, and it's like no one notices you. Your demise is eminent, but here comes Jesus to bring you back to life. What a mighty God we serve. Just when you count yourself out, He comes and breathes new life into the situation. He resurrects you and brings you out of your tomb so that you can be a shining example of what God can do. Once God raises you up, you must tell others what He did. If you are in the middle of a dark situation, know that God is on His way. Don't despair; He will be there to resurrect you from the dead. Continue to pray and have faith, and watch Him work on your behalf. Today, remember that God is not going to let you die in your despair. He is on His way. Trust that God knows what He is doing. He cares for you and has your best interest at heart. He will bring you BACK TO LIFE.

Prayer

God, my present has literally sucked the life out of me. I feel like a walking zombie. I can't see my future anymore. My heart has so many wounds from people stabbing me that I'm fearful it doesn't even operate properly anymore. I'm sinking, and I need You to throw me a lifeline. I know that You have the power to turn my outlook around. I know that even in the chaos of my life, You can bring me back from the brink of death. I desperately ask that You give me a hot shot and charge me back up. I cannot do this for myself, Lord. I need You to do it. Please Father, bring me back to life, like You said You would do. Even if my situation stays the same, give me new life in the midst of it. I pray to You in faith, knowing that You will do this for me, Your child.

In Jesus' Name,

Amen

Listen To: "Before I Die" by Kirk Franklin

Thoughts and Ponderings

_____

_____

Day 19

GOD IS WITH YOU

Deuteronomy 31:8 (NIV)

The Lord himself goes before you and will be with you; he will never leave you nor forsake you. Do not be afraid; do not be discouraged.

You can never be reminded enough that God is with you. When you are facing life's most difficult situations, knowing God is with you gives you strength to make it through another day. As horrible as things may seem, remember that God goes before you. This means He knows everything that is going to happen, and He knows what lies ahead. You are human, so of course when faced with your harsh reality, you will become scared, frustrated, sad, upset, and maybe even hurt. However, you have to use your faith muscles and speak to that part of your human self. Tell yourself that God is with you and He didn't bring you this far to leave you in despair. He knows what's best for you and in time, He will reveal it all. As hard as it is, you must use your faith to get through this. Remember what Hebrews 11:1 states: "Now faith is the substance of things hoped for, the evidence of things not seen" (KJV). You've asked God to guide you, now use your faith and believe that He will give you the desires of your heart and answer your prayer. Do not be afraid, and do not be discouraged. God is with you, and will continue to be with you.

Prayer

Dear God, I feel so alone. This situation I am facing is taking its toll, and I feel like I am in this thing by myself. I know You are here, but I can't see You, I can't hear You, and I can't feel Your presence. I need You, Lord. Please make Your presence known to me, in any way that You deem appropriate, and when You do, please open my eyes and ears to receive it. God, I need You. There is no way I will make it through this without You. Be with me and everything connected to me, and when this is over, I promise to share the good news about what You have done for me.

In Jesus' Name,

Amen

Listen To: "Trust Me" by Richard Smallwood

Thoughts and Ponderings

_____

_____

_____

_____

_____

_____

_____

_____

_____

_____

_____

_____

_____

_____

_____

_____

_____

_____

_____

_____

_____

_____

_____

_____

_____

_____

_____

_____

_____

_____

_____

_____

Day 20

GOD IS A SHIELD

Psalm 3:3-4 (NKJV)

But You, O Lord, are a shield for me,
My glory and the One who lifts up my head.
I cried to the Lord with my voice,
And He heard me from His holy hill.

God is your protector and He shields you from so much. He makes sure you are protected and He encourages you at the same time. Today's scripture reminds us that not only will God protect you from things meant to take you out, but He will lift your head and listen to what you say to Him. The fact of the matter is that God knows all, and He knows exactly what you are dealing with and what you are going through. He knows that it's difficult for you, and He is shielding you from things that will make it worse. Think about it. You may be dealing with the loss of a loved one, and while you are grieving, miraculously things have been going better than normal at work. That's God shielding you while you mourn. Or maybe you avoided a car accident, even though you were so deep in thought you don't remember which way you even drove home. That was God shielding you because He knew you were distracted.

God will always shield you and make sure that during your hardship, you can still lift your head up. See, if you keep your head held low, all you see is your present situation. But lifting your head helps you see possibility, it helps you see that the sky is the limit, it helps you see that there is someone greater than you working things out. God knows that you don't have the capacity to keep your head held high during difficult circumstances, so He assures you that He will do it for you. The awesome part about this is, you know that God is giving you strength, but it also serves as a testimony to others who see you dealing with the difficulties of life with poise and precision. As the gospel-singing duo Mary Mary would say, "It's just the God in you." God is using you even now to be a witness of the sustaining power that He offers. Remember, God is shielding you, He is lifting your head, and He hears every prayer and cry you utter to Him. Keep pushing. God is here.

Prayer

Dear Heavenly father, today I thank You for shielding me. I can be so immersed in my problems that I forget that You are still working things out on my behalf. Thank You, Lord, for being who You are in my life. Thank You for lifting my head to see new possibilities when I am too weak to lift it on my own. God, even in this, help me to be a shining example to others that one can be sustained in life's difficult moments by Your power. If I just sit here and let my mind think over all I have been through and what I am going through, I can clearly see You at work. I see how You fought for my protection, sanity, and happiness. I see how You spared nothing to make sure I came out whole. Thank You, Lord. Help me to remind myself of this when things become too much to bear, and I will continue to cry out to You because I know You hear me and I know You will answer. Thank You for being my shield. I love You.

In Jesus' Name,

Amen

Listen To: "Thou Oh Lord" by Brooklyn Tabernacle Choir

Thoughts and Ponderings

_____

_____

_____

_____

_____

_____

_____

_____

_____

_____

_____

_____

_____

_____

_____

_____

_____

_____

_____

_____

_____

_____

_____

_____

_____

_____

_____

_____

_____

_____

_____

_____

_____

_____

_____

_____

_____

_____

_____

_____

Day 21

BE BOASTFUL

2 Corinthians 12:9 (NKJV)

And He said to me, "My grace is sufficient for you, for My strength is made perfect in weakness." Therefore most gladly I will rather boast in my infirmities, that the power of Christ may rest upon me.

God does things in His own unique way. His way always pushes us to be better and rely on Him. This scripture outlines just that. God is telling us that His strength resides in weakness. When life gets tough, it's easy to get weak from just trying to make it. However, God is saying that in these moments, His strength is made perfect. The awesome part about this is when you are at your weakest point, God's strength is resonating in you for all to see. Have you ever been sad, worried, or confused, and someone says to you that they admire you, that they don't know how you do it all? It's God's strength at work in you during your weakest moments. His strength allows you to keep going in the face of adversity and allows you to be a witness to others, showing what God can do with and through you.

Maybe while you are reading this, you are saying, "I am at my weakest point right now." If you are, be encouraged, God had you read this right now to remind you that His strength is working through you. It's sustaining you and giving you what you need to make it another day. Put a smile on your face, and be boastful about the strength God has given you. God's power rests on you!

Prayer

Dear Heavenly Father, thank You for giving me the grace to make it through one more day. God, each day is a fight to make it to the finish line. I am often amazed how I get up each morning to tackle a new day filled with new emotions and issues, but I now realize that Your strength is operating in me and through me. When I feel weak, You make me strong. You know that I could not make it without Your strength. I don't know when You will remove me from this situation, but please continue to give me Your strength. I know I will come out victorious because of You.

In Jesus' Name,

Amen

Listen To: "Strength" by John P. Kee

Thoughts and Ponderings

_____

_____

_____

_____

_____

_____

_____

_____

_____

_____

_____

_____

_____

_____

_____

_____

_____

_____

_____

_____

_____

_____

_____

_____

_____

_____

_____

_____

_____

Day 22

BE JOYFUL

Romans 12:12 (NIV)
Be joyful in hope, patient in affliction, faithful in prayer.

This scripture provides a simple blueprint for dealing with hard moments in life. Be joyful in hope. Being joyful is a state of mind. It has nothing to do with your circumstances. Being joyful means you hold on to the fact that things will get better, no matter how dire the situation may be. It is a decision you make to keep a positive attitude and a hopeful spirit no matter what. This doesn't mean you will always be happy, but you will be hopeful. Be patient in affliction. This is much harder than it seems, but it is necessary. You have no control over anyone but yourself, so be patient. God is in control, and you have to let Him work everything out in His time. You also have to be faithful in prayer. Tell God what is on your heart—your hopes, dreams, fears, requests. Let Him know all of it, and then actively listen and wait for His response. Be joyful while you wait and pray. Remember the **joy** of the Lord is your strength, so while you remain joyful, He will give you strength.

Prayer

Dear God, thank You for this day. Help me to change my outlook regarding this difficult place I am in. I know You are with me. Help me to focus on that. Help me to remember that seasons change and this too shall pass. I strive to remain joyful in this current situation I face. I know that You will work things out for my good. I trust You and I believe in You, God. Thank You for hearing my prayer.

In Jesus' Name,

Amen

Listen To: "Joy" by Georgia Mass Choir

Thoughts and Ponderings

_____

_____

_____

_____

_____

_____

_____

_____

_____

_____

Day 23

YOU HAVE A TESTIMONY

Luke 8:38-39 (NIV)

The man from whom the demons had gone out begged to go with him, but Jesus sent him away, saying, "Return home and tell how much God has done for you." So the man went away and told all over town how much Jesus had done for him.

Things may seem bleak right now, but one day, God is going to turn your entire situation around. When He does, don't keep it to yourself; spread the word about what He has done in your life. By sharing your story, you encourage others. You show them that God can do anything because He did it for you. You become a billboard for the miracle working power of God. Quite often, part of the reason why we deal with certain situations is to reach back and help someone else. Don't miss your opportunity to help someone because you don't want to share. You should be so happy about what God has done that you shout it from the rooftops. Remember, God is going to bring you out of this, and once you are out, inspire others in their season of struggle and hardship. Be a living example of what God can do. Sometimes all it takes is to hear that someone made it through to give you the strength to endure. You can be someone's last chance at holding on. Don't take it lightly. Share the good news of what God can do. Remember, you always have a testimony. Even while going through a test, you have a story of what God has done in your life.

Prayer

Dear Heavenly Father, thank You so much for all that You have done in my life. I'm going through a hard time right now, and that tends to consume my thoughts, but today I chose to think about past victories and all that You have brought me back from. Thank You for giving me a testimony about Your goodness. Help me to get to the other side of this so I will gain yet another victory to boast about. Thank You for always keeping Your word. I am believing by faith that this time will be no different. I will get through this and You will get all the glory.

In Jesus' Name,

Amen

Listen To: "Testimony" by Anthony Brown and group therAPy

Thoughts and Ponderings

_____

_____

_____

_____

_____

_____

_____

_____

_____
_____
_____
_____
_____
_____
_____
_____
_____
_____
_____
_____
_____
_____
_____
_____
_____
_____
_____
_____

PERSEVERE!

James 1:4 (NIV)
Let perseverance finish its work so that you may be mature and complete, not lacking anything.

You've heard all the clichés: good things take time, diamonds are developed under pressure, God won't give you more than you can bear, and the list goes on. These may be true, but they don't help you when you are in the middle of the pressure zone, not knowing how long you will have to stay there. It gets so hard that you ask God to remove the situation entirely so that you will be happy again. However, your prayer needs to change. Don't ask God to take the situation away, ask Him to give you strength to endure it. Today's scripture encourages you to persevere. It may be hard, it may be hopeless, but stay the course so that once it is done, you will come out of the trial stronger and wiser, having learned everything that God intended you to learn. God will give you the strength to persevere.

Prayer

Dear God, I know You are all powerful and can do anything. However, You have not changed my situation. I've been praying and praying for change, but You haven't answered. So Lord, if I have to endure this, please help me to learn the lessons You are teaching so that I don't ever have to visit this space again. Let me be stronger and more mature once this trial is over. Give me the strength to learn and endure while I wait on You to turn my circumstance around.

In Jesus' Name,

Amen

Listen To: "Finish Strong" by Jonathan Nelson

Thoughts and Ponderings

_____

_____

_____

_____

_____

_____

_____

_____

_____

_____

_____

_____

_____

_____

_____

_____

_____

_____

_____

_____

_____

_____

_____

_____

_____

_____

_____

_____

_____

_____

_____

_____

_____

_____

_____

_____

_____

_____

_____

_____

_____

_____

Day 25

BE OF GOOD CHEER

John 16:33 (NIV)

I have told you these things, so that in me you may have peace. In this world you will have trouble. But take heart! I have overcome the world.

It would be great if life was always happy, easy, and fun. It would be perfect if things always went as planned, your feelings were never hurt, and the sun was always shining. As wonderful as this would be, it's just not reality. John 16:33 reminds us that we will face trouble in our lives, but we need to take comfort in knowing that trouble comes to everyone. If this is a rough season for you, find comfort in the fact that trouble is a part of life. You are not alone in this struggle. There is hope for you.

Whatever you are dealing with, Jesus has already overcome it. He has already defeated it. You just need to keep pressing and pushing through to make it. It's normal to worry and feel scared when facing the unknown. However, Jesus tells us to have peace—a peace that others may not understand, but will sustain you through the unsustainable. It is possible to be happy, even in the midst of sorrow. God has taken care of whatever may be bringing you down. Spend time with Him and allow being in His presence to lift your spirit so you can be happy again.

Today, while you face life's adversities, do so with peace in your heart. Be of good cheer because Jesus has already taken care of it.

Prayer

Lord, please grant me peace to endure this storm. I know You have everything in control. I know in the end I will come out victorious because of You, but right now I don't feel that way. Honestly God, I just want to be happy again. I know this is possible. Today, remind me of all the reasons I have to be happy. Let me remember that You, above anything else, bring **joy** and happiness to my life in the best and worst of times. Let me find my contentment in You. I'm trusting You and I love You.

In Jesus' Name,

Amen

Listen To: "Happy" by Tasha Cobbs

Thoughts and Ponderings

_____

_____

_____

_____

_____

_____

_____

_____

_____
_____
_____
_____
_____
_____
_____
_____
_____
_____
_____
_____
_____
_____
_____
_____
_____
_____
_____
_____
_____
_____
_____

Day 26

GOD IS WORKING!

1 Peter 5:8 (NIV)

Be alert and of sober mind. Your enemy the devil prowls around like a roaring lion looking for someone to devour.

Fighting through the battles of life can leave you weak physically, mentally, and spiritually. When you are at your lowest and weakest, the devil will see you as the perfect target. He will begin to prey on your insecurities and make you doubt yourself and doubt what God has said to you. You must stay prayed up and seek God even when you don't have the energy to do so. Surround yourself with people that will pray for your strength in the Lord. Feed your spirit with scripture, Christian music, and positive thoughts. Do whatever you can to safeguard yourself against the enemy. Ask God for discernment so you can tell who God has sent to help restore you and who the devil has sent to tear you down. God knows the devil wants to take you down, and He is working on your behalf to ensure that you come out victorious. Stay alert because the devil is looking to take you down, but don't worry because God is working.

Prayer

Lord, I need Your help and Your strength to stay alert and fight off the enemy. I know the devil would want nothing more than to see me defeated, but I am determined to overcome. This evil is ever present, it's everywhere, and the devil will use anyone and everyone to deter me from my future. God, I need Your protection. Help me to avoid the landmines and pitfalls planted by the enemy. I know I have the victory. God, just help me to endure until I see it.

In Jesus' Name,

Amen

Listen To: "I've Seen Him Work" by Anita Wilson

Thoughts and Ponderings

_____

_____

_____

_____

_____

_____

_____

_____

_____

_____

_____

_____
_____
_____
_____
_____
_____
_____
_____
_____
_____
_____
_____
_____
_____
_____
_____
_____
_____
_____
_____
_____
_____
_____
_____
_____

Day 27

YOU WILL SOAR!

Isaiah 40:31 (NKJV)

But those who wait on the Lord
Shall renew their strength;
They shall mount up with wings like eagles,
They shall run and not be weary,
They shall walk and not faint.

Waiting is so hard. The most difficult part of waiting is not knowing when the waiting period is over. You spend most of your time wondering, *Is this the end? Is my wait over?* You consume yourself with worry. Isaiah 40:31 says not to worry while waiting. It is during the wait that you are renewed. The defining aspect of this scripture is that you are waiting on God, not circumstances or the ability of someone else. Waiting on anything or anyone but God will deplete your energy. However, if you wait on God and Him alone, He will renew your strength so that when you come out of your situation, you will be unstoppable. Think about it: eagles are strong, they fly at high altitudes, and they soar alone. God is telling you that you will soar, you won't get tired, and you won't faint if only you wait on Him. Change your perspective on waiting. Instead of worrying, get excited because God is restoring you and renewing you in this season. Get your affairs in order, and write out your dreams and plans, because when God changes your season, you will hit the ground running and you won't get tired.

Today, follow His direction and wait for Him to change the situation around. God is worth the wait, and your life will never be the same. Get ready to soar.

Prayer

Dear God, I'm in a season of waiting. This is so hard because I don't know how long this season will last. I have so many questions, and I want to take matters into my own hands and handle it my way. God, please send reminders that I am right where I am supposed to be. I'm going to walk in my renewed strength until it's time for me to soar. I'll look for ways that You are sustaining me, and I will focus on that instead of everything I cannot control. Please increase my faith so I can soar for You.

In Jesus' Name,

Amen

Listen To: "They that Wait" by Fred Hammond

Thoughts and Ponderings

_____

_____

_____

_____

_____

A Joiful Moment

_____
_____
_____
_____
_____
_____
_____
_____
_____
_____
_____
_____
_____
_____
_____
_____
_____
_____
_____
_____
_____
_____
_____

Day 28

YOU ARE STRONG

Nehemiah 8:10 (NIV)

Nehemiah said, "Go and enjoy choice food and sweet drinks, and send some to those who have nothing prepared. This day is holy to our Lord. Do not grieve, for the joy of the Lord is your strength."

If you have been in church for any amount of time, you have heard a portion of this scripture repeated several times—"The joy of the Lord is your strength." It's wonderful to quote—empowering even—but it's slightly difficult to grasp. How is the **joy** of the Lord your strength when you are battling things left and right? How is the **joy** of the Lord your strength when you are at your lowest?

Think about how this applies to your life. When I look back at my lowest moments, I see how the **joy** of the Lord strengthened me to keep going. God revealed His **joy** in the little things—waking me up, keeping me healthy, watching over my son. These seem like minor daily tasks, but I was enduring so much at the time that even these tasks seemed major. They gave me **joy** and allowed me to keep my hope and faith in a God that provided **joy** on a daily basis. This **joy** helped sustain my faith and made me stronger. I didn't even realize how strong I was becoming until my season changed, and I was no longer in the grips of despair. I was able to see how God's **joy** strengthened me and helped me focus on something other than my circumstance. You may not realize it now, but you are strong because the **joy** of the Lord is and will always be your strength.

Prayer

God, thank You for Your **joy** that is revealed to me daily. Heighten my awareness so I can see the areas in my life where You are working and building me up to be a better person and better Christian. I want nothing more than for You to get the glory out of this. Keep me focused on You and only You. I praise You even now for what You are going to do through me.

In Jesus' Name,

Amen

Listen To: "The Joy of the Lord" by Coko Clemons

Thoughts and Ponderings

_____

_____

_____

_____

_____

_____

_____

_____

_____

_____

_____

_____

_____

_____

_____

_____

_____

_____

_____

_____

_____

_____

_____

_____

_____

_____

_____

_____

_____

_____

_____

_____

_____

_____

Day 29

JOY

Psalm 30:5 (NKJV)

For His anger is but for a moment,
His favor is for life;
Weeping may endure for a night,
But joy comes in the morning

Maybe you're facing the hard truth that the difficult situation you're enduring right now is totally your fault. You took matters into your own hands and made a mess of things. Now you have to figure out how to make things right. You may even feel distant from God right now because of your actions. Psalm 30:5 assures you that God's anger is but for a moment. Forgive yourself and move on knowing that God does not hold a grudge toward you. No matter how you arrived in the situation that you're in, it won't last forever. Weeping may endure for a night, but **joy** comes in the morning. We never know when our morning will arrive, but we have faith that it will come. While you are in your weeping season, it will seem dark and lonely. You may not be able to see where you are going–you may even lose your sense of direction. But keep praying, keep reciting scripture, and keep reminding yourself what God has said about you. Eventually you will see the sun start to rise over the horizon, and you will know that morning is on its way. That light may be a song or sermon you hear, or a hug, or just the firm realization that God didn't bring you this far to leave you. Just remember that no matter how dark your night is, **JOY** is on the way.

Prayer

God, it's dark right now—really dark in my life. I feel the storm winds blowing. I'm lost, and I don't have any idea how everything will turn out. Please be by my side, and help me hold on until morning comes. I know that this is a season, and it will change, but I need You in order to endure. Be with me God, and most importantly, help me to recognize morning when it comes. My eyes are adjusted to the darkness, so much so that the light just may frighten me. Send me spiritual sunglasses so I won't be shocked when You send Your morning light.

In Jesus' Name,

Amen

Listen To: "Joy" by Vashawn Mitchell

Thought and Ponderings

_____

_____

_____

_____

_____

_____

A Joiful Moment

_____
_____
_____
_____
_____
_____
_____
_____
_____
_____
_____
_____
_____
_____
_____
_____
_____
_____
_____
_____
_____
_____
_____
_____
_____

YOU WILL BE RESTORED

I Peter 5:10 (NIV)
And the God of all grace, who called you to his eternal glory in Christ, after you have suffered a little while, will himself restore you and make you strong, firm and steadfast.

God has promised you so much, and in this verse, He promises to restore you after you have suffered. It may be impossible to even imagine good times again. You have been dealing with heartbreak and hardships for so long that it has become a way of life. Don't get used to it. Difficult situations are what God uses to build your faith and renew your trust in Him. It was never intended to be the culmination of your journey, but a stop along the way, so don't set up permanent housing. Allow yourself to be free from the weight of your current situation. Do the work while waiting on Him. Work on yourself, deal with your pain, forgive those that hurt you, develop a plan of success, and when God restores you, take off running with the strength He has given you.

Prayer

Dear God, thank You for never leaving me in my pain. I'm hurting right now, but I am encouraged by the fact that You are going to restore me. It helps to know that I am not wasting time, but I am being purposeful in waiting on You. Give me everything I need to be ready when You move. While I am dealing with my pain, help me to see where I need to grow and what I need to change so that You can use me. Thank You for showing me grace and for literally holding my hand through this season. It hurts, but I know it would hurt more if you were not here. Continue to be with me, and I promise not to forget what You have done for me.

In Jesus' Name,

Amen

Listen To: "Restoring the Years" by Donald Lawrence

Thoughts and Ponderings

_____

_____

_____

_____

_____

_____

_____

_____

_____

_____

_____

_____

_____

_____

_____

_____

_____

_____

_____

_____

_____

_____

_____

_____

_____

_____

_____

_____

_____

_____

_____

_____

_____

_____

_____

_____

Conclusion

You did it! You completed the thirty days of this devotional. It is my prayer that you are stronger in your faith and knowledge of who God is in your life. I hope that you can now see how God is holding you and guiding you through whatever situation you may face. He never misses an opportunity to get the glory out of your life. Don't be discouraged. Know that He has it under control, and you will come out better than when you went in. Allow what you know about God to conquer your human fears and anxiety. Don't let those feelings win. At the end of the day, God will not let you fail. Things may stray from your plan, but God always knows what's next. Trust Him like never before. All God requires is faith the size of a tiny mustard seed. Apply that small amount of faith to your situation and watch God water it and grow it to be even larger than you thought capable. You can do this! Remember, don't lose your faith, and don't let anyone steal your **JOY**!

Acknowledgements

I have to thank God for bringing me through the unimaginable to get to a point where I can encourage others to get there too. While I grew up learning about God, there is nothing like experiencing God's power for yourself. He has a funny way of teaching and reinforcing lessons, but I am glad I have experienced Him in a personal way.

To my son, WDIII, I love you so much. When I didn't have the strength to get up for me, I remembered that you were depending on me and I couldn't give up. You were my reason until one day I became my reason. I love you forever, son.

To my parents, Bishop Walter and Lady Patricia Thomas, there really aren't enough words to adequately express what you both mean to me. Thank you for your example of Christian living. Thank you for introducing me to God. I wouldn't have made it through if you didn't take your job seriously. I love you both so much, and I know I would not be the woman I am without you.

To Walter, Jarrette, Joshua, and Candice—my squad! You all are my siblings and forever friends. Thank you for your listening ear, for drying my tears, for spending time with me so I wouldn't be alone, and for just loving me. To my other babies, Lillian, Walter III, Ava, and Baby Joshua, you all are my bright spots. I love being your Auntie.

I want to thank the rest of my family, including the Thomas family, the Lyles family, the Moore family, the Drummond family, and the Stewart family for your unconditional love and support. To my God family, the Majors, I love you all. Thank you for loving me back.

There are a few people I have to mention that have helped me and been a shining example of what it looks like to come through your trial. Special thanks to Rotunda Jenkins, Raymel Mosley, Shannon Moore, Glenda Boone, the Debnam family, the Garrett family, Dr. Dianne Roberts, Michelle Williams, Diann Cupid, Morgan Waller, DeEtta Roberson-Carter, Avalon Taylor, and Cassandra Vaughn. Love ya'll.

I have to acknowledge my best friend of over 20 years, Godlee Davis. Thank you for always being there, listening, and giving me sound advice. Love you.

To my church family, New Psalmist Baptist Church, the best church on the planet! Thank you for loving me, covering me in prayer, not judging me, and always having my back. I'm grateful to call you my one and only church home.

To my WEAA "Gospel Grace" family—Derryck, Jamal, Tyra, Mark, Ernestine, and Bass—thank you for always supporting me. Love ya'll.

I want to acknowledge my godfather, Min. David Major, who I miss dearly. I hope I'm still making you smile.

I must also acknowledge my grandmother, L. Elizabeth Thomas, who passed while I was completing this devotional. There isn't a day that goes by that I don't think about you. I remember what you told me when we discussed my divorce and I hold on to those words to this day. I love you!